31 Days of Praying for Your Future Husband

How the power of a praying woman can
change her future marriage

Caitlyn Burns

Valued and Esteemed Publishing

31 Days of Praying for Your Future Husband: How The Power Of A Praying Woman Can Change Her Future Marriage

Copyright © 2017 by Caitlyn Burns
Valued and Esteemed Publishing

ISBN 978-0-996-91791-9

Unless otherwise indicated, all Scripture quotations are taken from the Holy Bible: New King James Version. Copyright © 1979, 1980, 1982, by Thomas Nelson, Inc. Used by permission. All rights reserved.

Scripture quotations marked (KJV) are taken from the *Holy Bible*, King James Version. Used by permission. All rights reserved worldwide.

Scripture quotations marked (NLT) are taken from the *Holy Bible*, New Living Translation, copyright ©1996, 2004, 2007, 2013 by Tyndale House Foundation. Used by permission of Tyndale House Publishers, Inc., Carol Stream, Illinois 60188. All rights reserved.

Scripture quotations marked (NIV) are taken from the *Holy Bible*, New International Version®, NIV® Copyright ©1973, 1978, 1984, 2011 by Biblica, Inc.® Used by permission. All rights reserved worldwide.

Cover Design: Caitlyn Burns
Cover Photo: Unsplash
Editor: Lauren Gayoso
Interior Layout: Caityn Burns

Printed in the United States of America

To my future husband whom I have been patiently praying for and to every woman who is still waiting for God to bring her future husband

table of Contents

Introduction

Prayers For Your Future Husband

Traveling Through My Journey Of Praying

I am so excited to share a journey that God has taken me on since I was young. The very first time I remember praying for my future husband was right around the age of twelve. Looking back, I can't believe how early I started praying for him, but I think that God had impressed upon my heart the desire for marriage—specifically a marriage that would honor and glorify Him!

Even though I started praying at age twelve, my prayers were few and very far between. However, once I finished high school the reality of marriage became all the more real as friends started dating and one by one were getting married.

It's kind of funny to think that for all these years I have been praying for a man that I have yet to meet. One day when I do marry my future husband, I can't wait to hear all about what God has been doing in his life during the time I was praying for him.

There have been times in my prayer life that have flourished and then times when discouragement or the doubt of ever getting married began to set in. But, I know the Lord has specifically placed this desire for marriage in my heart and prompted me to be praying for my future husband and the marriage that we will one day share.

Praying for your future husband can start right now! When I pray for him I pray for anything that comes to mind or whatever the Lord impresses upon my heart. Praying for him can just be a simple thing you share with the Lord, or if you want, you can write down your prayers in a notebook, or in a card. The Lord is working on your future husband's life as well as your life right now. You have no idea of the power of prayer! Not only does it strengthen and encourage your walk with the Lord, but your prayers for your future husband will benefit him as well.

It may seem silly at first, but I have found that the more and more I pray for my future husband, the more and more I realize I am witnessing the Lord work in my life first hand because of my prayers. It has been amazing to watch friends who have prayed and waited for their future husbands now getting married to the man whom they have been praying for. This is God's beautiful love story unfolding in His perfect timing. Start praying for the man God has for you and watch as He unfolds your love story in His perfect timing. It is never too early to begin!

The Power Of A Praying Woman

How often do we underestimate the power of prayer? I think that we underestimate the power of prayer in our lives because there is not an immediate result from our prayers. Sometimes, God has us praying for the same situation for years and other times the prayer seems to be answered overnight.

The power of prayer is beyond anything that we can even begin to imagine and there is amazing power when we pray in the name of Jesus! In each circumstance in our lives, our first instinct should be to bring it all to Him in prayer. Even though we have all seen the power of prayer at work in our lives at some point, how often is prayer our last resort instead of our first priority?

One of my favorite songs is, "What A Friend We Have In Jesus" by Joseph M. Scriven. There is a specific reason this is the song that I think about when I am praying. One of the lines in the song goes:

What a privilege to carry everything to God in prayer,
What a peace we often forfeit,
Oh what needless pain we bear,
All because we do not carry,
Everything to God in prayer.

The entire song is all about taking our prayers to the Lord. Can you imagine how different our lives would be if we made prayer our first instinct instead of viewing it as a last resort? I believe that we would see lives changed—specifically ours—in ways that we could never imagine! God can do amazing work in your life through prayer and all you have to do is allow Him. Prayer is not a one-time act, but a lifetime filled with diligent prayers. The journey of walking with our Savior is meant to be a journey that is filled with prayer.

Think about prayer as a garden. If you were to start a garden, first you would till the ground to get it ready for planting. After caring for the soil, you would then tenderly place all the flowers inside of the ground and water them with just the perfect amount of water. Each day after, you would patiently watch for the flowers to begin to bloom. You would make sure to pull out any weeds at the first sight of them. As the days pass, the flowers would bloom beautifully because of all the care you have put into the flowerbed. Each flower has been groomed to perfection and there is no sight of any weeds or tares in the ground. You have taken care of the garden you planted and now you are seeing the labor of your work with the flowers blooming ever so beautifully.

Prayer is indeed like a spiritual garden in our lives. The more that we pray and seek God the more our garden will grow. We need to pull out the *weeds* of doubt, bitterness, anger, discontentment, and hopelessness and replace all of those *weeds* with His heart, His character, and the fruit of His Spirit.

I pray that your garden will be filled with love, joy, peace, patience, kindness, goodness, faithfulness, and self control. All of those qualities are ones that we so desperately need in our lives now, as well as in our future marriages. We need them and so do our future husbands.

There have been so many times when I have underestimated the power of prayer—the power of prayer regarding my own life situations and the lives of others, including my future husband's. It's easy to think that it's really not that big of a deal or that my prayers may not have any influence at all. I know that all of this is just the Enemy whispering into my ear trying to distract me from what the Lord has called me to do as my husband's future wife, which is to pray for him.

There is never anything too big or too far into the future that we can't begin to pray for right now! Just think if your future husband were to tell you that for years he has been praying for you. Praying for the marriage you will one day have. Praying for your character. Praying for your walk with Christ. Praying for the woman that God is preparing for him.

Waiting For The Unseen Future

God knows exactly who your future husband is! He knows every single little detail about your future man's life even before he was born. Darling, God knows everything about you too, including the cries of your heart. Do not give up or give in to the Enemy's tactics to discourage you from praying for your future husband. Keep pressing forward.

There is a verse in Galatians that has greatly encouraged my heart when the discouragement sets in and when I think I can no longer continue to pray because all I seem to hear is "wait". The verse says, "And let us not grow weary while doing good, for in due season we shall reap if we do not lose heart" (Gal. 6:9). I know that it can be extremely difficult to be patiently waiting for God to bring you your future husband, but patience is a fruit of the Spirit. While you are waiting and praying for your husband, do not become discouraged if God hasn't introduced you to him in just a few months, or if the months turn into a year, or if the year into many years. God's timing is perfect! His ways are far beyond our ways.

As a single woman myself, I understand the pain of your heart's cry when you have been praying for years with still no prospect of a future husband. But, I can only tell you that even through my seasons of discouragement or through my tears of pain, I know that God is working on my heart just as He is working on my future husband's.

The one thing that has kept me praying after all of these years—five years on a consistent basis—is that God has taught me how to pray through this process. If you don't know how to pray, then ask God to teach you how to pray as you pray scripture, blessings, and God's will over the life of your future husband.

Our journey of praying for our future husbands is not over once the wedding day arrives, but rather is just a new chapter in our prayer lives. Instead of praying for your future husband, a man with no name and a timeline with no date, you are now praying for your long-anticipated husband—the man God brought you and the man that is now your life-long husband. The new chapter of prayer begins when you become husband and wife. Now, you are praying over your marriage and the future you will share together. It is no different than when you were praying for your future husband except that you now have a specific person to pray for!

Our prayer life should not be a one-time prayer experience, but must be a lifetime of prayers! If you are single, dating, or soon to be married, I pray that you will be encouraged to start praying for your future husband right now. That you would begin to intercede on his behalf and for all that the Lord wants to do in your future marriage.

Part of what praying for your future husband entails is that you will leave your love story up to God. You will not be perfect on your journey of prayer, or letting God write your love story, or even trusting God in bringing you your future husband. What it does mean is that you are willing to go against what the culture says, "Just live for the now," and instead, you will live for the future God has planned for you—knowing that the impact of your actions right now will affect your future husband and marriage one day.

Prayer has been one of the most affective ways of growing in my Christian walk. Some prayers get an answer right away with the exact answer that I have prayed for while other prayers take time. Prayer is a spiritual discipline that comes with time. I have not grown in my prayer life or my relationship with God based on just a prayer at dinner. The times that I have grown the most is through having prayed and then being told by God to wait. So, I would wait, and wait, and wait. The more I waited and prayed, the more my faith grew because I knew that God would answer me in His perfect timing.

I pray that this book would be an encouragement to you to start praying for your future husband and that you would see the power of your prayers come to life. I hope you will see God's hand at work and that you will fully come to understand the power of prayer. Just know that I am praying for my future husband along side of you and you are never alone in this journey.

How to Use The Prayers

I am so excited to begin this journey of praying for our future husbands together! It is something the Lord has placed on my heart and I am excited to share this journey with my sweet sisters!

Here are a few ideas of how to use these prayers:

1. Read these prayers for your future husband during the next thirty-one days.
2. Read each prayer out loud every day.
3. Write down each prayer in a journal or on a note card.
4. Use the journal on the opposite side of the prayer for each day to write your thoughts or your own personal prayer.
5. Save your journal or note cards to give to your future husband on your wedding day.

There are so many different ways to use this book, but above all, I pray that it encourages you to pray for your future husband. The power of prayer is more than we can see right now, but it will forever affect the future.

After each prayer there is a page where you can journal. This is a place for you to add your own thoughts or personal prayers. The prayers aren't just for you to use and then leave, but rather a starting point of helping you to begin praying for your future husband.

Never underestimate the power of prayer and how God can change lives through the prayers you pray! He wants to do amazing things in your life and all you have to do is be willing. So be willing— start praying for your future husband right now!

I can't wait for you to read this book and to one day be able to share with your future husband that you have been praying for him! I can only imagine how special that will be for him!

Day One
Walk with the Lord

Heavenly Father,

I pray that my future husband's walk with You would be strong. I pray that You would give him a heart and a love for You like nothing else in this world. Nothing will ever be able to compare to the love You have given him. May You always be his first love and I pray he would keep You as his first love all the days of his life. As he loves You more and more, I ask that he would seek You and desire to have a deeper relationship with You—a relationship that will never grow cold or stagnant, but one that would be steadfast and unshakeable. Give him a walk with You that is only more solidified with each day and with each moment that he spends with You. Help him to run the race—his walk—with endurance. Don't allow him to give up, but help him to keep pressing onward to the goal set before him, which is Christ Jesus.

May he be a man who spends time to hear from You each day, who reads Your word, and listens to Your voice. May he long to sit at your feet and hear your instructions. Give him a desire for You above everything else in this world. This world can be so discouraging, but may he keep his eyes and heart focused upon You and the promises You have for his life. Don't allow him to grow weary in his walk, but encourage him and bless his life for following You. Surround him with other believers who will encourage him in his walk with you, Lord.

Keep his heart wholeheartedly steadfast upon You. Fill his life with blessings because he has chosen to faithfully follow You all the days of his life. When times become difficult may You be his rock, one he can cling tightly to knowing that You are using him for Your glory. Allow his love for You to pour out of everything he does. Shape and mold his heart to be more like You each and every day.

Amen!

"Therefore you shall lay up these words of mine in your heart and in your soul...for if you carefully keep all these commandments which I command you to do—to love the Lord your God, to walk in all His ways, and to hold fast to Him." —Deuteronomy 11:18, 22

Journal

_____

_____

_____

_____

_____

_____

_____

_____

_____

_____

_____

_____

_____

_____

_____

_____

Day Two
Commitment

Lord Jesus,

In a world where we break our word to those around us, may he be one who keeps his word. Allow his "yes" to be "yes" and his "no" to be "no". Mold him into a man who is known for keeping his word and commitments with others.

When you direct him toward the next step in his life, allow him to commit to whatever is before him. Don't allow him to get distracted from his commitments, but to faithfully keep to the task at hand. May he remember to be faithful in the small things in life as well. Give him the ability to keep focused on the commitment that is right in front of him and to not be distracted because another good thing comes along. I pray the man You have for me would desire to keep his word, no matter what everyone else says or is doing. I ask that you would mold and shape him and I into men and women who stand strong in our commitments.

Jesus, may he also be a man who is waiting for his future wife. Keep his heart safe and secure for our future marriage. May my future man be one who will be committed to us, and our marriage, for the rest of our lives—until death do us part. Commitment in marriage does not begin once marriage starts, but it begins right now. Give him eyes to see that his life of commitment right now is preparing him for a lifetime of commitment in marriage—in his walk and in every area of his life.

Thank you in advance for preparing a man for me whose heart is steadfastly committed to all You have placed before him. Keep his heart loyal to his earthly commitments and to the most important one, the commitment to his walk with his Heavenly Father and Savior.

Amen!

"Let your heart therefore be loyal to the Lord our God, to walk in His statutes and keep His commandments, as at this day." —1 Kings 8:61

Journal

_____

_____

_____

_____

_____

_____

_____

_____

_____

_____

_____

_____

_____

_____

_____

Day Three
Desires of His Heart

Heavenly Father,

I love that You have specifically placed desires in the heart of my future husband. Just thinking about all that You will do in his life one day amazes me. Father, thank you for giving him desires deep within his heart, ones that he may know right now and ones that You will bring to light later in his life.

As he delights himself in You through reading Your word, praying, serving, and seeking You, allow his desires to come alive in his life. First and foremost, I ask that my future husband would seek Your will and desires above his own. May he want to please You more than he wants the desires of his heart.

Whatever desires he has within his heart, let them be desires that You have given him. You have called him individually to do great things. Help him to not just sit still for You, but help him to move every little piece in his life for Your glory. Give him an end goal for his desires, but take my future husband's hand and lead him each step of the way. The path from where he is right now, to where You will have him in the future, is not going to be a direct path—it will be one that has twists and turns. Help him to trust You each step of the way and to enjoy the journey.

Breath life into his hopes and dreams. Even though his desires may not work out exactly the way that he thought, fill his heart with so much joy because he is doing exactly what You have placed in his heart.

Thank you, Father, for giving him desires, hopes, and dreams for the future. May he delight in You all the days of his life and see You move mightily in his life through the desires You placed in his heart.

Amen!

"Delight yourself also in the Lord, and He shall give you the desires of your heart." —Psalm 37:4

Journal

_____

_____

_____

_____

_____

_____

_____

_____

_____

_____

_____

_____

_____

_____

_____

_____

_____

Day Four
Protection

Father,

There is so much violence and evil in the world. Each and everyday we are surrounded by evil and people with evil intentions. Lord, protect my future husband from any harm that might come his way. Shield him from the Enemy's fiery darts and surround him with Your protection.

Father, I pray that you would give him spiritual protection as well as physical protection. He does not wrestle against flesh and blood, but against the rulers of darkness. Surround my future husband with Your protection from spiritual, physical, mental, and emotional attacks and watch over him. I pray that you would be with him today in all that he does. Father, establish and guard him against all harm that might come his way. I pray for protection in all that he does. Father, may he daily put on Your armor like a warrior ready for war. Keep him on guard and alert to the enemy's tactics. Equip him for each battle that he faces and help him to know that he is not alone in the fight and that You are right there beside him.

It is easy to let your guard down when you are exhausted, but I pray that my future husband would find strength to keep going despite the battles that he is facing. If the attacks are physical, please keep him healthy and strong. If the battles are spiritual, equip him with the sword of the Spirit to fight with. If the battles are mental, bring friends into his life who will encourage him and I pray that he would find security in Your love letter to him.

While I do not know right now if the battles he is facing are spiritual, physical, mental, or emotional, You do. You know exactly what he needs protection from. Equip him to face the battles and challenges standing right in front of him. Prepare him to be a man who seeks protection from You, and You alone. Thank you for constantly watching over him!

Amen!

"But the Lord is faithful, who will establish you and guard you from the evil one."—2 Thessalonians 3:3

Journal

_____

_____

_____

_____

_____

_____

_____

_____

_____

_____

_____

_____

_____

_____

_____

_____

_____

Day Five
Humility

Father,

It takes a great amount of character to have humility. It is so easy to be prideful and to want to make ourselves look better. I pray that my future husband would be a man who allows You to honor him. Even when those around him are discouraging him from establishing character in his life, be right there with him encouraging him to stay humble and focused. Give him the wisdom to know how to act with humility.

Lord, allow him to be different than the world around him. Your word says that we are to value others above ourselves. This is not always an easy task and he can't do it without Your help. May he desire to emulate You because you humbly became a servant for us. As he seeks to serve those around him, overflow his heart with love for those around him. Give him a heart that is willing to do anything—even the tasks that no one else wants to do because he knows that he is serving You.

There will be times when he will get prideful or when the ministry You have called him to grows beyond his ability to stay humble. Continually give him circumstances in life that will cause him to stay humble. I pray that he would not be a man who boasts about his accomplishments in this world, but he would rather boast about all that You have done in and through his life.

There is always a trait to be worked on and sanctification will never be completed. Pride comes before a fall, but may he not say or do anything that would bring destruction to his life. All the days of his life may he desire to practice humility. Thank you for constantly working on *this* character in my own life and in the life of my future husband. Thank you for your perfect example.

Amen!

"Therefore humble yourselves under the mighty hand of God, that He may exalt you in due time." —1 Peter 5:6

Journal

Day Six
Wisdom

Heavenly Father,

We know that wisdom is precious. Lord, I am asking that you would grant my future husband wisdom that comes from You. You say in Your Word, that in order to receive wisdom all we have to do is ask of You and You will give it liberally (James 1:5). Lord, I am asking for Your wisdom, in faith, that you will shower my future husband with Your wisdom from above.

The world thinks it has wisdom to offer, but it does not. The wisdom of this world is not the same as the wisdom that comes from you. The wisdom of this world is fleeting, but Your wisdom will last forever. As he goes through life, grant my future beloved with Your wisdom. Help him to make decisions based upon Your will for his life. May he seek Your advice and wisdom above all the counterfeit wisdom the world has to offer. Give my future husband discernment to know the difference between the wisdom of the world and wisdom from You.

There are so many areas in life that we need godly wisdom. Surround my future husband with parents who will guide him in the Lord and with friends and mentors who will impart godly wisdom into his life. Wisdom is not just getting advice, but knowing what to do with the advice given. Help him not to rush right into the advice he has been given, but rather weigh this advice and align it with Your wisdom and Your word. Allow him to accept whatever wisdom or truth You reveal to him.

Whatever life decisions he so desperately needs wisdom on, I ask You would give him your unending wisdom. Lord, when you give my future husband wisdom, I pray that he would not be become boastful or wise in his own eyes. Keep his heart humble.

Amen!

"If any of you lacks wisdom, let him ask of God, who gives to all liberally and without reproach, and it will be given to him." —James 1:5

Journal

_____

_____

_____

_____

_____

_____

_____

_____

_____

_____

_____

_____

_____

_____

_____

Day Seven
Character

Lord Jesus Christ,

My future husband is not only so dear to my heart, but even more so to Your heart, Lord. His reputation and character goes so much further than he will ever be able to see. Give my future husband character that will speak of who he is and display that he is different because of You. May he be a light brightly shining in the darkness for You. There are so many situations where our character can be easily compromised. Let him stand for You even in these situations because his character and walk is more important to him than anything else. Surround him with friends who share the same character.

May integrity and honesty be a large part of his character. Bless him for his desire to establish character that is pleasing to You. Help his character to stand strong against the tides of the culture. I pray for the man he is today, for the man he will be tomorrow, and the man you are making him into for the future. Continue to mold and shape my beloved into the man You are making him to be. Through every season of life, Lord, may You be the one who is refining the rough edges of his life and shaping them into a life that is more like You. Do the same with his character. Mold, shape, and refine his character through his day-to-day life and through the seasons of blessings and trials.

His character can measure the quality of who he is because sometimes all you know about a person is based on their character and reputation. Allow his character to speak for itself and for his character to be proven over time. When coworkers, friends, or family members question who he is, may his character stand trial even under fire. There will be people who will try to accuse him or try to trip up his character, I pray that when this happens my future husband will stand strong as he walks with integrity.

Amen!

"Giving all diligence, add to your faith virtue, to virtue knowledge, to knowledge self-control, to self-control perseverance, to perseverance godliness." —2 Peter 1:5-6

Journal

_____

_____

_____

_____

_____

_____

_____

_____

_____

_____

_____

_____

_____

_____

_____

_____

Day Eight
Testimony

Jesus,

You have given my future husband a testimony, one that is to be used for Your glory. Every single blessing, trial, hardship, and joy is part of his testimony. Nothing that he has gone through is for a waste and I thank you for using his life and his story for Your glory.

May his life be a living testimony of Your grace and forgiveness in his life. Give him opportunities to share his testimony with others on a regular basis. His story is all part of the picture that You have painted for his life. His life is also part of a living testimony of who You are. May he never be ashamed to share the story of his testimony.

I don't know the full details of his testimony, but You do. Remind him that he has never gone too far for You to use his testimony. In whatever platform You allow him to share his testimony, give him wisdom to know what to share and how to share it. It may seem scary the first time that he is sharing it so give him boldness to speak.

In all that my future husband does, allow the testimony of Your love in his life to shine brightly. May people see his life as an example of how You can use someone as unlikely as us and how we can change the world through You. He has no story without You. You are his story and the reason that he has a testimony.

Help my future husband not to compare his testimony to others around him. If he doesn't think that he even has a testimony, show him exactly how You have used his life for Your glory and that is a testimony by itself. There are so many more pieces to his testimony than he even realizes. You have given him his testimony for a reason and you have equipped him to share it with others.

Amen!

"And they overcame him by the blood of the Lamb and by the word of their testimony, and they did not love their lives to the death." —Revelation 12:11

Journal

_____

_____

_____

_____

_____

_____

_____

_____

_____

_____

_____

_____

_____

_____

_____

_____

Day Nine
Emotions

Jesus,

Thank you for the gift of emotions. At times it can seem like a blessing and a curse, but Lord, we know this ability to express ourselves through our emotions comes from You. There will be days when my future husband and I don't handle our emotions correctly and we are sorry for that. May we desire to learn how to display our emotions in a way where they won't control all that we do, or hinder us from thinking correctly, or using proper discernment.

Emotions are a precious and wonderful gift. They help us to see how others are thinking and feeling and allow us to express our feelings as well. Help my future husband and I to be vulnerable with our emotions toward each another and with those we love. It's not an easy thing to be vulnerable and to display our emotions. Give my future husband and I the ability to be honest and real with each another even when it's difficult. Jesus, when he is feeling joyful or excited, allow those feelings to come from the depths of his heart. When he is anxious or nervous, allow him to feel Your presence surrounding Him and for Your peace to flood his heart. I pray that when he feels amazed at all You are doing in his life that it will be a testimony he can share with those around him.

Give me, as his future wife, the ability to help him through times when his emotions get the best of him or when he does not understand why he is feeling a certain way. I pray that he would not see emotions as a hindrance, but would see them as a blessing. Give him a heart of compassion toward me when my emotions are running free and help him to understand when I do not know why my emotions are running free. Thank you for the ability to have emotions and the ability to express them to those around us. I pray that he would enjoy all the emotions that life brings.

Amen!

"A time to weep, and a time to laugh; A time to mourn, and a time to dance."
—Ecclesiastes 3:4

Journal

Day Ten
Relationships

Heavenly Father,

You gave us the gift of having relationships. Thank you for this gift of being able to have a friendship with You and those around us. Develop a relationship between my future husband and You that will grow deeper and deeper with time. Direct him toward You and keep his eyes fixed upon the most important relationship in his life—the one he has with You.

Father, I ask for the relationships he has in his life right now. I pray they would be ones that honor and glorify You. Strengthen his relationships with his family, friends, and coworkers. Allow these relationships to be an encouragement to him. May these friends be ones who can lift him up in prayer and give him wise counsel when he needs to make decisions.

The relationships we have with our family members and with each other are the ones that will be the most important to us. I pray that my future husband would be a man who loves his family and would love our future family. Make him into a man who invests in his family and the relationships that are important—the relationships that will affect him his whole life.

I am so excited for the future relationship You have planned for my future husband and I. May we always keep You as the most important relationship in our lives together. Marriage is a commitment to one another *until death do us part* and a great marriage will take time and effort to keep it working. Give us the type of relationship that learn to stand the test of time despite all we may face together as a couple. Thank you, Lord, for all that you are going to do through the relationship we will one day share together.

Amen!

"Two are better than one, because they have a good reward for their labor...though one may be overpowered by another, two can withstand him. And a threefold cord is not quickly broken." —Ecclesiastes 4:9; 12

Journal

_____

_____

_____

_____

_____

_____

_____

_____

_____

_____

_____

_____

_____

_____

_____

_____

Day Eleven
Contentment

Lord Jesus,

The things of this world are so tempting and can easily distract us from You. I pray that You would place Your contentment inside of my future husband's heart. Lord, may he be perfectly and peacefully content exactly where You have placed him right now. May he not look to the right or to the left, but would keep his eyes and heart fixed upon where You have led him. In whatever season of life You have him in right now, teach him what it means to be truly content. When life does not work out his way or the way that he planned, show him that You are in control. Teach him that this is part of learning to be content when You shut doors and when You take him in a new direction.

Paul learned what it was like to be content, whether he had little or much, and I pray the very same thing for my future husband. It is difficult to be content in all things, but I pray this quality would be one my future husband is constantly working to achieve. He has been so blessed by You. Help him to remember to thank you for all You have given him.

Even though we are not together yet, allow both of us to be content in the season of singleness You have placed us in. Don't allow distractions to take us away from enjoying the season You have placed directly before us. Your plan is perfect! Help my future husband and I to trust your plan at all times and in all seasons. Thank you for his season of singleness—a time when he can focus on You and grow in his walk with You. In all circumstances and in all seasons of his life, give him a heart that is overflowing with contentment.

Amen!

"I am not saying this because I am in need, for I have learned to be content whatever the circumstances. I know what it is to be in need, and I know what it is to have plenty. I have learned the secret of being content in any and every situation, whether well fed or hungry, whether living in plenty or in want."
—Philippians 4:11-12 (NIV)

Journal

Day Twelve
Guarding His Heart

Lord,

You have called my future husband to guard his heart—being careful on what he allows into his life and the influences that may affect his life. His heart is so precious and valuable. The heart is what life comes from. Help him to know the value of his heart and the importance of guarding his heart. Solomon wrote in Proverbs 4:23, our hearts determine how we live.

I ask that my future husband would learn how to guard his heart. Provide him with the discernment to know what to share with others and what is only to be kept between You and him. When others try to get him to leave his heart unguarded, help him to see that guarding your heart isn't just for today, but it is a lifetime of work. Teach him how to guard his heart and show him the value of keeping his heart guarded. Guarding himself begins in the heart and then it flows into every other area of his life. Lord, allow him to see that guarding his heart doesn't mean that he can't share with others or show emotions, but that he should be careful to weigh advice given to him and be careful to determine what he allows into his life.

In his relationships, give him the ability to keep his heart guarded until our wedding day. May he not be too quick in giving his heart away, but would rather keep it secure in You. It can be easy to want to give your heart fully to someone. Help him to use discernment in deciding when to open up his heart to me and to know when the time is right. As his future wife, I ask that You would help him to stay steadfast in You during our relationship and our marriage. Thank you for teaching both of us the value of guarding our hearts! Thank you for his diligence in learning to guard his heart.

Amen!

"Guard your heart above all else, for it determines the course of your life."
—Proverbs 4:23 (NLT)

Journal

Day Thirteen
Integrity

Jesus,

Our culture doesn't value integrity the way it should. Each day there are so many opportunities presented where my future husband can choose integrity. I pray that when he is faced with chances to show integrity that he would choose integrity. May his example of integrity be one that makes him stand out from the culture and may others know it's because of his walk with Christ.

Jesus, You know his character and the desires of his heart. I pray that my future husband's heart would be one that constantly desires to do what is right. Allow his heart to be solely steadfast and undivided on what You have placed in his heart. Draw him closer to You as you lay Your way of integrity before him.

Proverbs 10:9 says, we are to walk with integrity all of our lives. I know it is not always easy to walk the path of integrity, but I pray my future husband would desire to follow Your example of integrity as long as he lives. May he not compromise his integrity and convections despite the situation directly in front of him. I ask for integrity in his work life as well. There will be circumstances where he can either turn the other way and ignore the issue, or he can stand up and address the issue. May he desire to walk in integrity in those difficult circumstances because he is a man who is grounded in You and the morals that You have given him as an examples to live by.

Bad things happen when godly men do nothing. I pray that my future husband would be an example of how when godly men live with integrity that evil will no longer triumph. Surround him with godly men who will set the example of what it is like to walk with integrity. Bless his life for desiring to follow the biblical morals set before him, for living a life filled with integrity, and for desiring to do what is right in Your eyes. Help him to learn from Your perfect example!

Amen!

"He who walks with integrity walks securely..." —Proverbs 10:9a

Journal

_____

_____

_____

_____

_____

_____

_____

_____

_____

_____

_____

_____

_____

_____

_____

_____

_____

Day Fourteen
Vision

Father God,

Your Word describes how without vision the people will perish (Proverbs 29:18a). I pray that my man would be a man of great vision. Equip him to accomplish all You have given him to do. May he be an effective tool for You and for Your kingdom. Whatever vision You have given him for the future, I pray my future husband would be willing to follow that vision. Sometimes, Your vision can be scary because it leads to the unknown. Sometimes, Your vision can be exciting because You are opening doors. Give him the wisdom to hear Your voice and to see Your vision.

When he is confused on the plans in front of him, grace him with Your will and vision. Clarity is from You and You alone. Your word says that You are not a God of confusion, but of peace (1 Corinthians 14:33). Fill his heart and soul with Your peace to fulfill the hopes and dreams instilled deep within him. Those hopes and dreams that are for the future and for right now.

Father, you have great and wonderful plans for him and for our future family. I pray that You would already begin providing him with a passion for the work you have prepared before him, in advance, so that he may walk according to your will. Thank you for allowing him to be a part of Your wonderful and mighty plans. I pray that in all of his plans that You would be the first one that he seeks counsel from when deciding where You would have him go. Open his eyes and heart to see what Your vision for his life is. Help him to be willing to follow where You lead him.

In whatever position You place my future husband, may he have a vision and a plan. Lead and guide him each step of the way as he walks according to Your vision and calling for his life. Give him faith to see beyond the present and to see the wonderful future ahead!

Amen!

"Where there is no vision, the people perish." —Proverbs 29:18a (KJV)

Journal

Day Fifteen
Leadership

Heavenly Father,

Thank you for the gift of leadership, specifically spiritual leadership. I pray my future beloved would be a man who is strong in spiritual leadership. Instruct him in how to lead and to lead by example. As he walks closer to you, plant and grow the gift of spiritual leadership in his heart. Leading others can be difficult and challenging. Encourage my future husband to lead in the positions You have placed him in right now. When he is leading others let that be an opportunity to grow the leadership abilities he has and to instill new ones in him.

I am excited for him to be able to lead our house and family one day. May he make time to spend with You, to hear from You, and to listen to You, so that he may lead our family in the right direction. There will be days when he feels like he has failed—pick him up and help him to keep leading. Don't allow the Enemy to discourage him from leading our family closer to You.

Help me to be a supportive wife and to allow my future husband to lead. Allowing him to lead in every area that You have called him to and that he would know that I will be there to encourage him in the leadership opportunities ahead of him. When he fails or feels like he has fallen short in his leadership, help me to have the right words of support and encouragement for him. Thank you for creating me to be his biggest cheerleader and his biggest supporter in all areas of his life, especially leadership.

Take his hand and lead him closer to Your heart. Father, I pray that my future husband would be a man who leads our family spiritually. I pray that he will have godly men in his life whom will encourage him in how to lead our future family. Give him a love for You so that he can lead us and our family with diligence and love. Thank you, Lord.

Amen!

"Let no one despise your youth, but be an example to the believers in word, in conduct, in love, in spirit, in faith, in purity." —1 Timothy 4:12

Journal

Day Sixteen
Calling

Abba Father,

I thank you for the calling You have placed in the life of my future husband. I pray that You would encourage him in the calling You have placed in his heart and on his life. There are so many distractions in the world and things that can draw him away from the calling You have specifically placed on his life. Give him the courage to follow his calling even when others are discouraging him. Provide him with a peace that surpasses all understanding, knowing that You are the one who gave him this calling.

Father, I don't know what the calling on my future husband's life is, but You do. I thank you for calling him and preparing him for the task that You have set before him. Cause his eyes not to wander to the right or to the left, but to keep steadily pressing onward toward the goal You have placed before him. I pray that you would equip him for the journey You have called him to. Give him the wisdom to follow where You are leading him and to place the opinions of others to the side and only listen to Your leading. Allow my future husband to be found worthy of the calling that You have placed before him.

Encourage him in the calling that is set before him and I pray he would not measure himself according the world's standard. I pray that You would give him the ability to trust You even when his calling is challenging or when he does not understand why You have this specific purpose for his life. When he is confused and does not understand why you have placed this calling on his life, I pray that you would confirm his calling to him. Give him the assurance that you are the one who called him before he was born. Do not allow fear or intimidation to set in, but help him find boldness and courage in You and in Your word. May he live to please You in all that he does.

Amen!

"The eyes of your understanding being enlightened; that you may know what is the hope of His calling, what are the riches of the glory of His inheritance in the saints." —Ephesians 1:18

Journal

_____

_____

_____

_____

_____

_____

_____

_____

_____

_____

_____

_____

_____

_____

_____

_____

Day Seventeen
Purity

Abba Father,

I don't think that we can ever fully grasp the importance of purity. The purity in our lives flows into so many other areas. Father, purity doesn't stop after my future husband and I get married, but rather it is a lifestyle. I ask that my future husband would grasp the importance of saving himself for marriage and the importance of purity in his heart and thoughts.

Sexual purity is the one that weighs heaviest on my heart, Father. Our world doesn't value the importance of waiting until you are husband and wife or even the love that it provides within the context of marriage. I pray that my future husband would be different than the culture around him. Give him a heart that understands the importance of purity. Help him not to be in situations where his purity has a chance to be compromised.

Sin is only pleasurable for a moment, but it can reap a lifetime of regretful consequences. Keep his heart safe and secure in You when he is tempted to let go of his purity. May my future husband's life be an example of purity—encouraging others to fight to keep their purity and to stand firm against the ways of this worlds. You know the struggles that he faces every day. Help him to overcome those struggles through You and help him to strive for purity.

Father, I ask that my future husband would desire not just sexual purity, but also purity in his heart and mind. I can only image the struggle my future husband faces each day. Protect his eyes from images of women who are inappropriately dressed. Place men in his life who will help keep him accountable, but most importantly, help him to remember that he is accountable to You. Thank you for helping him live a life of purity as he walks according to Your word.

Amen!

"How can a young man cleanse his way? By taking heed according to Your word." —Psalm 119:9

Journal

_____

_____

_____

_____

_____

_____

_____

_____

_____

_____

_____

_____

_____

_____

_____

_____

_____

Day Eighteen
Witness

Lord Jesus,

You were and are the perfect example of what a witness is to look like. I pray my future husband would desire to be a strong witness for Your kingdom. May his life be one that brings honor and glory to Your name. Don't let anything around him or the world extinguish the flame for You that is shining brightly in his life. Let the light shine so brightly that others may see the love he has for You and they would wonder what is different about him. Provide him with the right words to say when he is questioned about the life he lives and give him an answer for the light that lives within him.

Living a life for Christ requires that he is continually a witness for You in every single part of his life. There will be a difference about his life because of how he strives to live according to Your Word and Your example. Allow him to have friends who are non-believers who are watching his witness and notice there is something different about him through his actions alone. Give his life salt so that he is a living example of how Christ can change a person's life. In every area of his life, including: school, work, friends, ministry and family, I ask that he would be an example to those around him—living a life that is evidently different than the culture and world. Let the evidence of his walk with Christ be so strong in his life.

Thank you for the ability to share Your word and Your love through our actions. May we always be lights shining brightly in a dark world. Give my future husband the words to say when he is asked why he has this hope inside of him, which is because of You, Lord. Help him to have the answers to the questions that may be asked and I pray it would be Your words and not his. Thank you for being the perfect example of what a witness looks like and how to be a light to those around us.

Amen!

"Let your light so shine before men, that they may see your good works and glorify your Father in heaven." —Matthew 5:16

Journal

_____

_____

_____

_____

_____

_____

_____

_____

_____

_____

_____

_____

_____

_____

_____

_____

_____

Day Nineteen
Past, Present, and Future

Heavenly Father,

The past is exactly what it is—in the *past*. Whatever happened in my future husbands past, I pray it would stay in the past. Do not allow whatever has happened in his life before Christ, or even while he was walking with Christ, to be a hindrance in his life. When he confesses the past, give him the wisdom to understand that You have forgiven him as far as the east is from the west and that you remember it no more. If the past still has a hold on his life, Father, please give him victory over allowing the past to be in the past. Victory can only come by confessing his past and allowing You to heal the broken pieces of his life. The Enemy may try and do all that he can to not allow my future husband to truly let go of the past, but I pray the Enemy would not have a foothold in this area of his life. You are the only one who can turn a life around, make him whole, wash him anew, and forgive him.

It can be easy to wish for a new season or to dwell on the future. Help my future husband to live life to the fullest because he has You right by his side. Cause his life, right now, to be filled with You. Whatever season he is currently in, let Your light shine so brightly in his life. Draw him closer to You during this present day. Thank you for using him exactly where he is right now. Pave the way for his future by preparing him each step of the way with his current situations.

The future can be so exciting, but it can also make us anxious. The fear and anxiety of the future can be scary, but give my future husband peace that You have the future in Your hands. There is so much to plan for the future and so many possibilities of how You can work in our lives. You have so many wonderful plans for his life. Help him to trust You with the unknown and to live in faith.

Amen!

"Do not remember the former things ,nor consider the things of old. Behold, I will do a new thing, now it shall spring forth; Shall you not know it? I will even make a road in the wilderness and rivers in the desert." —Isaiah 43:18-19

Journal

_____

_____

_____

_____

_____

_____

_____

_____

_____

_____

_____

_____

_____

_____

_____

_____

_____

Day Twenty
Physical Health

Lord,

Each and every breath that my future husband takes is a gift from You. He cannot do anything without having taken a single breath. Thank you for giving him life and for allowing him to wake up each morning. Lord, You are in full control over my husband's health and over every single cell in his body. Give his body the ability to fight whatever virus comes into his body and give him a body that is physically healthy.

I don't know the journey that is ahead of us in our marriage. I don't know if my future husband will have cancer one day, if he will get ill on a regular basis, or if he will be fighting different health battle—only You know the future, Lord. I ask that You would give him a strong healthy body. He needs a healthy body to be able to provide for our family and be a part of our family. I ask that he would be able to play with our future children and be a part of their lives until they grow old. Allow my future husband's body to be healthy and I pray that every single aspect of his physical body you would keep in Your hands.

Help me to be a source of strength and comfort to my future husband in sickness and in health. It can be scary not knowing what the future holds, but I know that You hold the future. I ask that You would keep my future husband's health in Your hands. Lord, I don't know what you have planned for his life. I don't know if my future husband will be in good health for many years or if we will go through battles of sickness. In whatever state his physical health is in, I ask that You would be his strength. If he is sick, help him to cling to You in his illness and know You are in full control over his body. If he is healthy, then please keep him in great health. Thank you for the gift of health and everything my future husband can do because he is healthy.

Amen!

"Beloved, I pray that you may prosper in all things and be in health, just as your soul prospers." —3 John 1:2

Journal

_____

_____

_____

_____

_____

_____

_____

_____

_____

_____

_____

_____

_____

_____

_____

_____

_____

Day Twenty One
Role as a Husband and Father

Jesus,

The role that my future husband will have as a husband and father are roles that You have entrusted to him. There are so many aspects of being a husband and father. Teach him what it means to be both and how to balance them well. The amount of godly husbands and fathers is greatly decreasing in the world around us. I pray that he would be an example for the culture and that he would desire to be a husband who leads in the Lord and a father who is involved with his children. I ask that my future husband would desire to lead our marriage and our family in You.

First, I want to pray for his role as a husband. Whether his father was a godly role model or not, help him to be a husband who is the spiritual leader of our home—seeking to lead our marriage closer to You and to each other. When he is overwhelmed in his role as a husband, help me to be the helpmate who can come along side him. Strengthen him and equip him to be a godly husband.

The Enemy wants to cause division, especially in marriages. Help my future husband and I to be aware of the Enemy's tactics. Give us the ability to stand strong in our marriage and I pray we would be an example of a godly marriage to those around us. Place other couples in our lives that will be an encouragement to us and to our marriage.

Fatherhood is such a special gift that You have given. With each child that You give my future husband and I, give my future husband a love for each one that is like a caring father's love. A love that is selfless, only wants the best for his children, and is full of compassion, but also corrects and disciplines in order to train up our children. I pray he would lead our future family in the ways of the Lord so our children may grow up seeing Christ at the center of his life.

Amen!

"The righteous man walks in his integrity; His children are blessed after him."
—Proverbs 20:7

Journal

_____

_____

_____

_____

_____

_____

_____

_____

_____

_____

_____

_____

_____

_____

_____

_____

Day Twenty Two
Forgiveness

Abba Father,

"Forgive and let go." This phrase is so much easier to say than to actually do. God, help my future husband to truly forgive the people who have hurt him. Whatever they have done to him, allow him to let go of the pain they have caused him and the bitterness that he has held on to for too long. He can't forgive on his own. He needs Your help.

I pray that my future husband would not be a man who holds a grudge for a long time. Don't allow time to harden his heart and for bitterness to be stored up. When he refuses to forgive it only hurts his heart and life, holding him captive from truly living free in You. When it is hard for him to seek forgiveness, give him no other choice but to extend forgiveness. When his emotions are telling him that he doesn't need to forgive someone or that they don't deserve to be forgiven, give him the strength to forgive.

Father, You have forgiven him again and again. Thank you for Your example of how we are to forgive others. I ask that my future husband would look to Your example and that he would choose to forgive because You have forgiven him. Help him to walk in freedom, not being weighed down by the chains of bitterness that once held him captive. May he find complete freedom knowing that forgiveness begins in the heart and in the mind.

After he has forgiven those who have hurt him, when he later sees them, allow him to feel no bitterness or anger for their past actions. Give him the ability to move past the situation. Help him to continually choose forgiveness instead of bitterness. Help him to forgive those who have hurt him the most. Thank you for Your continual forgiveness in his life.

Amen!

"Bearing with one another, and forgiving one another...even as Christ forgave you, so you also must do." —Colossians 3:13

Journal

_____

_____

_____

_____

_____

_____

_____

_____

_____

_____

_____

_____

_____

_____

_____

_____

_____

Day Twenty Three
Boldness

Jesus,

Daniel is such a great example of boldness in the face of death. He was willing to obey You over the threat of death. You gave him incredible boldness to follow You. I pray that my future husband would exemplify the same kind of boldness—a boldness that is unwavering in its convictions and stands for truth. May he not fear man because he knows that You are with him in what You are directing him toward.

Wherever You are calling my future husband to go, give him the boldness to follow Your plan above his own—trusting in Your plan and in Your ways. You may call my future husband to have boldness in the plans that You have for him, maybe because the plans won't make sense to him at the time. When the plans seem bigger than he can even imagine and when the path You are directing him toward seems intimidating, give him the boldness to not be overwhelmed, but follow You. Enable him with the strength to boldly follow You where You may call him.

Preaching the gospel in any capacity requires boldness. Jesus, give my future husband boldness when he is sharing You with friends, family, and with those who don't know You. It can be difficult to share with those you are the closest to because they have seen you in all circumstances. Jesus, don't allow that to hinder my future husband from sharing what You did on the cross and how You paid the debt for their sins. Give my future husband incredible boldness to proclaim Your name to those who don't know You.

Jesus, let His love for You shine brightly when he is sharing the gospel with others. Thank you for giving him boldness, confidence, and courage because my future husband has allowed You to be his leader.

Amen!

"Have I not commanded you? Be strong and of good courage; do not be afraid, nor be dismayed, for the Lord your God is with you wherever you go."
—Joshua 1:9

Journal

Day Twenty Four
Spiritual Leader

Heavenly Father,

Leading our relationship, our marriage, and our future family is a tremendous task that you have given my future husband. Before we are even married and before we even have a family, may he strongly decided that he would serve the Lord.

Give him the desire to study to show himself approved so that he can be the spiritual leader of our home. I know this is a huge task and it may seem daunting at times, but fill him with Your Spirit and help me to extend grace when he is feeling like he just can't lead. I'm sure there will be days when he feels unequipped to lead our family spiritually. Equip him to be the spiritual leader that You have called him to be. Start preparing him right now and showing him the importance of being a spiritual leader. Fill his heart with the ability to tenderly lead our marriage and our family in the way that we should go.

So many marriages fail and homes are broken because there is no leader. Thank you that he does not have to lead alone because You are the one that he is following. May my future husband decide that he will lead our family regardless of what others are doing—standing up for righteousness, setting the example of following You, and being a man who prays before he does anything else. Place role models in his life who have gone before him and will help him grow.

Mold him into a man who has a heart like David, a love and desire to follow You like Paul, faith abounding like Abraham, a relationship with You like Enoch, and a boldness to do whatever You have call him to do like John the Baptist. All of these men, and many more, were spiritual leaders in their own day and in whatever capacity You placed them in. Thank you for calling him to lead our family! Encourage and equip him to be the strong leader that You have called him to be.

Amen!

"Choose for yourselves this day whom you will serve...but as for me and my house, we will serve the Lord." —Joshua 24:15

Journal

Day Twenty Five
Finances

Lord Jesus,

Finances and money can be such a temporary thing, but it is what we need to live on. I pray that whether we have much or whether we have little, that my future husband would be thankful for all that You have provided. In whatever season of life he is in right now, let contentment fill his heart and life. The things of this world are temporary. You look at the heart and You long for him to desire a heavenly treasure instead of an earthly reward.

Finances can sometimes be short and he may have no idea where the next paycheck is coming from. Give my future husband the ability to trust You, the Lord who provides for His children. Your word says that he will never be lacking what he needs. He may not always have what he wants, but You will always give him exactly what he needs. When the finances are short, I ask that You would cause him not to worry about where the money will come from, but he would trust in You alone for his provisions. When we rely upon You in faith, You answer in ways that we could never expect! Bless his job so that he may be able to provide for himself and for our future family.

Jesus, help my future husband to have the wisdom to know how to budget and plan for the future as well as right now. Focusing on only today can cause harm later on with finances. May he be wise with his money and how he spends it. Supply all of his needs according to the riches that are in You. Teach my future husband to always look for a way to bless others with Your money and that he would continually give back to you. Give him a willing heart to give to others who are in need. Allow the finances that he makes to be used for You. Thank you for all that You have given him!

Amen!

"But in the living God, who gives us richly all things to enjoy. Let them do good, that they be rich in good works, ready to give, willing to share, storing up for themselves a good foundation for the time to come, that they may lay hold on eternal life." —1 Timothy 6:17-19

Journal

Day Twenty Six
Pursuits

Lord Jesus,

A life that pursues Christ can encompass so many different areas. You have instilled in my future husband's heart the desire to purse goals and dreams. Allow the goals and dreams that he pursues to be ones that align with Yours.

May my future husband desire to pursue a relationship with You above anything else in this world. Each morning when he wakes up and as he begins a new day may he seek You in all that he does and in his plans. He can accomplish nothing if he is not in constant pursuit of You. You are the one who will show him how to pursue godliness, righteousness, patience, and all the qualities that will make him a man after Your own heart.

As his future wife, I ask that You would give him the desire to pursue me. That You would make it so clear to him, when the time comes, to pursue a wife and marriage. Jesus, give my future husband the desire to pursue me, as his future wife, and continue pursing me even after we are married.

I know that my future husband has dreams and goals for the future. Plant the ability to pursue those dreams and goals that are within his heart. Pursing doesn't always come easily and he may get discouraged that it is not working out. Provide him with the encouragement to continue pursing the dreams and goals that You have placed in his heart.

Thank you for helping my future husband to learn how to pursue. May he always look to You above anything else and may he learn what it means to have a heart that pursues You and Your character.

Amen!

"But you, O man of God, flee these things and pursue righteousness, godliness, faith, love, patience, gentleness." —1 Timothy 6:11

Journal

_____

_____

_____

_____

_____

_____

_____

_____

_____

_____

_____

_____

_____

_____

_____

_____

Day Twenty Seven
Communication

Heavenly Father,

Communication is something that my future husband uses each and every day. Not only in how he conveys his words, but also in his actions and expressions. Communication is so important because it is how he expresses every single detail about his life to others. It is not something to take lightly. May he understand the incredible power that his words have. He has the ability to build a person up or to tear them down just by the words that he chooses to use.

I pray that he would be working on his communication skills right now. Communication is so vital to the flourishing of any relationship, especially in a marriage relationship. When he doesn't feel like communicating with me, give me the understanding to be the one to communicate with him. Father, when we are upset with each other, give my future husband and I the humility to admit where we have gone wrong. Help us to be quick to forgive each other.

Teach him to use his words well and I pray that his words would be encouraging and uplifting. We don't always understand the power of our words, but I pray that my future husband would see the impact of his words before he speaks them. If words are said in haste or in anger, show him where he was gone wrong and help him to seek forgiveness for those words. Harsh words can stir up anger, but soft words can turn away wrath. May he seek to speak in soft words and be slow to speak.

The words that he or I speak against each other can bring a lifetime of hurt. Help us to choose our words carefully, let our words be seasoned with grace, and allow only words that are encouraging and uplifting to fill our mouths. James 3:8 says that no man can tame the tongue, but I ask that You would help my future husband to tame his tongue.

Amen!

"Let your speech always be with grace, seasoned with salt, that you may know how you ought to answer each one." —Colossians 4:6

Journal

_____

_____

_____

_____

_____

_____

_____

_____

_____

_____

_____

_____

_____

_____

_____

_____

_____

Day Twenty Eight
Overcoming Temptation

Heavenly Father,

Oh, how the Enemy can be so trying! Every day my future husband faces temptation. The Enemy knows exactly what will cause him to fall and entice him to sin. Father, give him the ability to recognize the Enemy's tactics. Keep him alert and on guard to the Enemy's attacks.

I know that my future husband is not perfect and he will not withstand temptation every time. But, I ask that You would allow him to grow from his failures and he would not desire that temptation any longer. When he does fail, give him the ability to recognize his failure. The Enemy will use his failures to try to discourage him from standing firm the next time. I ask that You would give my future husband complete understanding to know Your truth and that it would set him free from temptation.

Thank you for the wisdom that You have given my future husband. Father, he needs wisdom from You in order to stand firm against temptation. There is no temptation in which You do not provide a way out or a way to say "no" to that temptation. While it can be easier to give in, instead of standing firm, help him to choose to stand firm instead of giving in to the moment of pleasure that sin provides. When he does fall, give him a heart that is truly repentant and longs to turn away from the sin, which can so easily ensnare him again.

Whatever it takes to help my future husband withstand temptation, I ask that You would make it happen. Strengthen him and equip him to combat the Enemy and to combat his fleshly desires. Thank you that he is not going through the battle alone, but that You are right there along side him.

Amen!

"No temptation has overtaken you except such as is common to man; but God is faithful, who will not allow you to be tempted beyond what you are able, but with the temptation will also make the way of escape, that you may be able to bear it." —1 Corinthians 10:13

Journal

Day Twenty Nine
Discernment

Lord Jesus,

The need for discernment is important in all of our lives. It gives us the ability to judge and weigh information—testing it for its credibility and worth. There is so much information in the world that is not beneficial for us. Help my future husband to have the wisdom and discernment to see through the deceit. It is so easy to be deceived by the words that we hear, but I ask that he would have ears that listen and a mind that exercises discernment.

Jesus, I don't know what his future job entails, but all I know is that he will need discernment when conducting business or when meeting with clients. Along with needing discernment in his job, he will need discernment in whatever capacity of ministry that he serves in during his life. Allow him to seek You and Your advice before moving forward in anything. I pray You would be the one to give my future husband a spirit of discernment. Regarding each decision that You place before him, give him discernment on which path to choose and which door to walk through. When he walks in discernment, flood his heart with peace.

Help him to be as wise as a serpent, but as gentle as a dove. Testing all the information that he receives and even those that he meets with. When he senses Your discernment telling him that something is not right, help him to follow through with the instinct You are giving him—not ignoring the warning, but following through by asking for Your discernment.

Thank you for giving him the ability to discern true from false, from godly men and men with hidden intentions, and being able to make judgments based on the instincts You have given my future husband.

Amen!

"Beloved, do not believe every spirit, but test the spirits to see whether they are from God, for many false prophets have gone out into the world." —1 John 4:1

Journal

_____

_____

_____

_____

_____

_____

_____

_____

_____

_____

_____

_____

_____

_____

_____

_____

Day Thirty
Patience

Jesus,

I know patience is one of the most difficult fruits of the Spirit. We want what we want when we want it. That's not how Your plan works though. Your timing is far better than ours and Your plan is far above anything we have planned. Help my future husband to trust Your timing and plans. Instill a heart and character of patience inside of him.

It is funny how we never pray for patience because we know that You will bring situations into our live that will cause us to grow in our patience. However, I ask that You would place my future husband in situations where You will grow his patience. Jesus, thank you for being so patient with my future husband. Thank you for never giving up on him while he is growing in his patience. I pray that he would desire to fill his life with patience. I pray that he would choose patience in situations where he is tempted to become angry or act on impulse.

When he looks to the future, may he see Your hand at work. Teach him to confidently wait with patience. Jesus, help him to be patient while you are working on bringing us together. May he patiently wait for me, his future wife. Keep him on course and help him to not look to the right or the left, but straight ahead. Allow him to wait with confidence knowing that You are at work in his life. Give him eyes and ears to see and hear Your heart and plan while he is in seasons of waiting. May my future husband be a man who runs the race steadfastly, pressing on while patiently waiting. Our walk takes time and patience to grow and to run the race you have set before us. Lord, give us strength, endurance, and patience while we press on toward the goal you have set before us.

Amen!

"But if we look forward to something we don't yet have, we must wait patiently and confidently." —Romans 8:25

Journal

_____

_____

_____

_____

_____

_____

_____

_____

_____

_____

_____

_____

_____

_____

_____

_____

_____

Day Thirty One
Strength

Lord Jesus,

You are all that my future husband needs. You are all that I need. When we are in times of weakness please be our strength—get us through the days and times when we just want to give in and give up. Renew his strength each day and I pray he would not grow weary while doing good.

Lord, remind my future husband that being weak is not a bad thing, for it makes him more dependent on You. When he is weak, help him to depend upon You for his strength.

When he is weak teach him to lean on You and gather strength from You. It is when we are weak that you teach us how to rely on You for strength. When he has rough days, ones that are physically, mentally, emotionally, and spiritually draining, provide him with the strength to press onward toward the goal you have set before him.

Lord, may we both desire to find our strength in You and You alone. Allow our strengths and weaknesses to complement each other so that we may be more effective as a couple. I don't know his strengths, but You do. I don't know his weaknesses, but You do. You alone are the source of our strength and You fill us in our times of weakness. You are the only one who can give power to him when he is weak. Help him to fully grasp the depth of the strength that can only be found in You.

Amen!

"He gives power to the weak, and to those who have no might He increases strength...but those who wait on the Lord shall renew their strength; they shall mount up with wings like eagles, they shall run and not be weary, they shall walk and not faint." —Isaiah 40:29-31

Journal

_____

_____

_____

_____

_____

_____

_____

_____

_____

_____

_____

_____

_____

_____

_____

_____

_____

Connect with Caitlyn

Blog: valuedandesteemed.com

Email: hello@valuedandesteemed.com

Instagram: valued_and_esteemed

Facebook: valued and esteemed

Made in the USA
Middletown, DE
01 September 2017